METAMORPHOSIS

FORM AND CHANGE IN THE ASHMOLEAN MUSEUM

FORM AND CHANGE IN THE ASHMOLEAN MUSEUM

XA STURGIS

Museums are of course places that encourage us to look at works of art but perhaps because within museums our senses are heightened, they are also great places to observe people; to look at the lookers. There is a long tradition, that stretches from Durer to Daumier and beyond, of pictures of spectators contemplating works of art. These often play on the relationship between the two and the echoes or contrasts between the viewer and the viewed, while at the same time they often deliberately blur the lines between the real and the represented. Works of art become animated as people assume the demeanour of statues or else the idealised world of art is contrasted to the imperfect and mundane reality inhabited by the spectator.

James Hudson's witty and visually intriguing photographs taken in the Ashmolean over 18 months from 2010–11 extend this tradition, capturing playful moments of symmetry and equivalence or contrast and dissonance as the public encountered the Museum's collection. James' photographs are also the portrait of a building, exploiting and evoking the character and detail of Rick Mather's ingenious reconfiguration of the Ashmolean that opened in 2009. Mather's building is built around the idea of interconnected galleries and spaces linked by glass-walled bridges that constantly offer glimpses from one space to another, enticing the visitor onwards and suggesting connections, both physical and intellectual, between different displays and collections. The photographs of *Metamorphosis* exploit to the full these glimpses and views, as well as the reflections offered by the glass walls and window-cases of the "new" Ashmolean.

But perhaps above all these works present a portrait of a living museum. The Ashmolean houses one of the country's great collections, with objects and works of art that span several millennia and continents. But the life of the Museum, and its purpose, is to be found in the encounters between the public and the collection. The photographs collected here are above all about these encounters. They naturally record a wide variety of possible responses to a museum, from slumped teenager to engrossed pilgrim. But in their imaginative and evocative picture-making, they also suggest the mystery of our relationship with the art of the past. For in our encounters with works of art, magic can happen and, like Ovid's heroes and victims, we can be transformed.

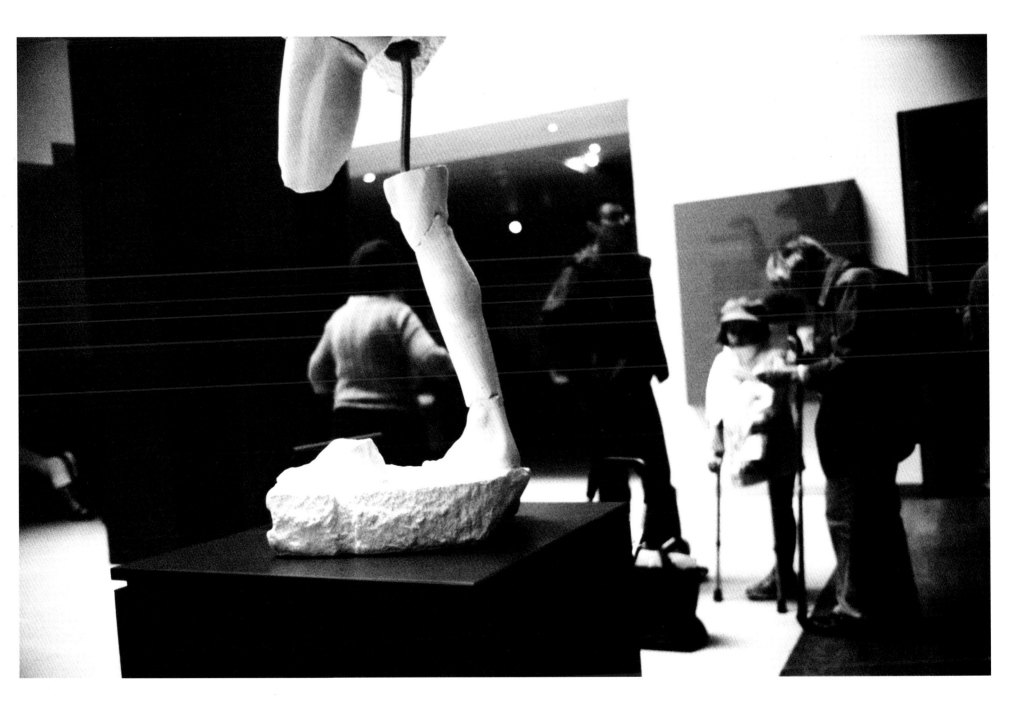

ZEUS AND ATHENA

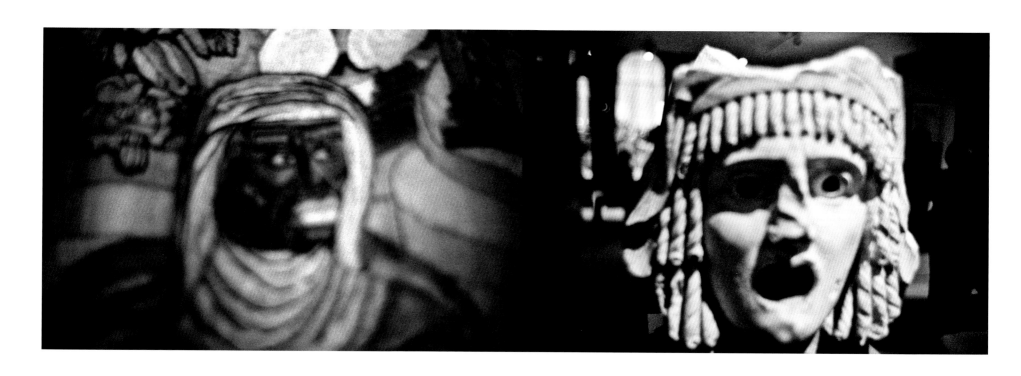

METAMORPHOSIS

JAMES A. HUDSON

It started out, like so many projects, with wandering. I'd moved to Oxford; the Ashmolean Museum had reopened after a multimillion pound rebuild, and I just wandered in. Almost immediately I started taking photographs somewhat surreptitiously — I was probably subject to the conventional wisdom that museums jealously guard the image rights to what they display. In an age when many people have a camera with them at all times, and with social media being a very simple and instant mechanism for publishing images, this seems an untenable stance to take. Only later did I realise that photography was not only permitted but actively encouraged by the Ashmolean.

People in museums often mimic the exhibits they are looking at, sometimes jokingly, as if they were mirrors, and sometimes completely unconsciously. I began to notice the interactions between the Museum's visitors and its new architecture, as well as between visitors and the objects on display. Out on the streets of Oxford, I was attracted to amusing situations, juxtapositions, shapes, light and decisive moments, and it was to the same sort of things that I was initially drawn in the Ashmolean.

Often the similarity between object and viewer was something I could only see from my particular vantage point — my subjects having no idea they were ever in such a relationship. Later, when I showed some of the work to the writer Heathcote Williams, he said it seemed that the "statues and portraits looked down at [the visitors] and all were fuelled for a piece of unconscious theatre". The boundaries between the visitors and the objects had started to overlap in the photographs. Glass cabinets started to contain visitors and not merely the objects. In fact, everything that I saw in the Museum became one of its objects as I wandered around, while the black and white film in my camera removed sound, movement and colour from the situations and shoved everything together into a 35 mm wide bit of plastic film drowned in chemicals. Heathcote didn't write that last sentence. But he did suggest that my growing collection of images was starting to resemble a "cabinet of curiosities" — Elias Ashmole's original title for his collection. Although I never really bought into that idea, several months later I decided to show my own version of the "cabinet of curiosities" to the Museum's press office.

There are no minutes from the meetings I had with the Museum staff, but the executive summary would probably read like something that could be printed on endless mugs, T-shirts and tea towels: "Have No Money and Carry On". So I did. To be honest, it would have been difficult to stop anyway; by now I was getting used to the building as I was there occasionally to photograph commercial assignments for the University, and also had to walk past the place most days. So I carried on for another year, going in several times a week. Sometimes I found a picture. Sometimes I left without a single click.

Although I had not been particularly interested in the actual history of the objects at the outset of the project, I started to read captions and eventually began to behave like many of the other visitors: consulting guide books, doing a bit of research, spending time on just one or two objects, being quiet, eating in the café, etc. This approach changed the work slightly as I became more embedded in the Museum rather than simply poking my camera at its surface.

At some point, quite far into the project, I remembered reading about statues coming alive and people being turned into inanimate objects in Ovid's stories of metamorphosis, and decided to reread some of them. In one story, Daphne becomes a tree, the American poet, William Wadsworth, describing her roots as spreading "… in secret to fascinate the rocks". In another story, Pyrrha and Deucalion create a new race of men from stones thrown on the ground. These changes in form happen over and over again. "Go out of the night whilst remaining in it" was how Marianne Van Hirtum described the phenomenon of metamorphosis and the more I read Ovid the more it connected with many of the photographs. The frustration caused by an inability to speak is also a recurring theme in Ovid's stories, and this related to what I was seeing in the Museum — quiet, often silent visitors and speechless objects.

Some of the photographs might look as if they are set up, but they are not. Nobody was ever asked to do anything in these pictures, for setting things up is usually connected to selling things in my experience. The girl on the gantry with her hands in the air, unknowingly mimicking the ancient miniature figures, was (I later found out) actually a dancer practising for a future performance in the atrium of the Museum. The religious persuasion of the man praying was first revealed to me at exactly the moment I took the photograph. And the young girl with one leg appeared only after many months of hoping something might happen near the important cast of the ancient one-legged statue of the fisherman. Wander, yes, but do be careful what you wish for.

JAMES HUDSON'S METAMORPHOSIS

PETER HAMILTON

A primarily photographic book such as this one is an expression of its author's wish to transform, or *metamorphose*, their photographic vision of the world into a publication. In this process of change, a subjective private vision mediated initially through the camera and the processes of photography, and later via the manufacturing process of printing, becomes transformed into a public object.

The term "photobook" has recently become common parlance to describe books like this one: the publication of a photographer as author of a coherent work with an expressive or documentary function, following the photographer-author's intentions. Latterly, they have begun to take on the status of art-objects in their own right, and to be collected as such, with values that are sometimes many multiples of their original sales price. Yet a paradox of history is that this very transformation was foreseen by those who envisioned photography in its beginnings. Indeed, the photographically illustrated book emerged almost simultaneously with the invention of the medium in the first third of the 19th century. One of these inventors was W. H. F. Talbot, the main client of his ex-assistant, Nicolas Henneman, who created a firm in Reading to demonstrate the utility of Talbot's negative-positive process for publishing, and produced his mentor's *Pencil of Nature* in 1844–6, illustrated with hand-made calotype prints. The book, issued as a part work to be assembled and bound by subscribers at its completion, was not a commercial success despite the novelty and beauty of its images — and even though, as Talbot wrote,

> The plates of the present work are impressed by the agency of Light alone, without any aid whatever from the artist's pencil. They are the sun-pictures themselves, and not, as some persons have imagined, engravings in imitation.

Though a commercial flop not helped by the technical difficulties posed by the print-making itself, the eleven surviving "complete" copies (for in fact the part-work was never brought to its intended

conclusion of a larger number of instalments) are probably by far the most valuable "photobooks" in existence. (Nonetheless, a copy of one of the mammoth "Sumo" volumes of Helmut Newton's work published in 1999 and signed by 80 of its subjects reportedly later sold at auction for almost half a million dollars, far in excess of the most recent auction price paid for a "complete" copy of *Pencil*.)

Looking back over the 170 years that connect James Hudson's *Metamorphosis* to W. H. F. Talbot's *Pencil of Nature* one is struck by the essential similarity of the two works. Quite apart from the obvious parallel that Hudson's Leica MP camera was using black and white negative film in an essentially similar way to that by which Talbot used his "mousetrap" camera to make his own paper negatives, both deploying a mechanical-chemical process that despite its huge development in the intervening period remains entirely analogous, the object of their enterprises was also surprisingly similar.

The role of photography, and thus of the photographer, is to transform objects, scenes, people, things, places into pictures that inform or invoke sense, meaning, and emotion. This is not the same as simply pointing a camera at something. There has to be a directing intelligence with an aesthetic or scientific intent, if the resulting picture is to be one that rewards, intrigues or satisfies. Talbot understood this dimension of his invention and foresaw that it would be of scientific as well as artistic value (and not merely because it would be the carrier of images in these two realms, or just a means to publish them).

Metamorphosis is a long picture essay about James Hudson's wanderings within the remnants of one of the most influential "cabinets of curiosities" ever created. Ashmole's collections (themselves largely based on those assembled by the Tradescants) are widely cited as key influences on the meaning, shape and form of the modern museum, and both his objects and their physical form of presentation — firstly in Oxford's Broad Street and later in the elegant Beaumont Street building of the 1830s — would also have been well-known to W. H. F. Talbot, who visited them during his scientific and photographic research, which has also left us the earliest photographic images of the city of spires. In addition there are numerous examples of Talbot's photography of similar types of objects to those that would then have been on display in Oxford. So Talbot and Hudson have followed similar paths.

But where Hudson and Talbot diverge, of course, is in their experiences of two very different iterations of the same museum, and of the results of the long history of photography since the mid-19th century. Hudson's work is situated quite clearly within a photographic tradition of street photography, where the ability of the small camera to capture ephemeral moments and juxtapositions offers the possibility of grasping, in a sixtieth of a second, transient expressions of metamorphosis. The contemporary museum is often (though not always) lighter and airier than its predecessor, but what is possible now in photographic terms means that the movement of the visitor within it and his or her engagement with its objects can be captured photographically in ways that would have amazed the British inventor of photography.

Perhaps it is a characteristic of the immersive form of photography engaged in by James Hudson, a sort of visitor's-eye view, but the pictures contained in this essay also suggest, strangely enough, an earlier vision of the role of the museum as a place of visual intrigue and curiosity, a place that contains exemplars of ennobling values and moral lessons, mixed in with the bizarre vagaries and oddities that life has somehow left stranded on the beach, as warnings against laxity. The visitor wandering through today's Ashmolean is still drawn in the main to the curiosities, visual delights and amusements on offer, rather than to the invisible mass of scholarship and documentation that lies beneath them, lurking like the submerged part of an iceberg. We are left with the intriguing idea that perhaps, and despite the transformations in the Museum that have occurred since the 17th century, the sense of metamorphosis experienced by its visitors may not be so very different.

ACKNOWLEDGEMENTS

A book of images from the project was always my ultimate goal, but for what has seemed like a very long time it did not appear possible. It certainly would not have happened at all without the encouragement and support of many other people, and therefore I would like to thank:

Susie Gault for her encouragement and for providing me with the residency to produce the work in the first place.

All the patrons of the book, but especially my parents and Bella Hobson for their generous contribution towards the production.

Paddy Summerfield, Patricia Baker-Cassidy, David K. O'Hara and Heulwen Hudson for their comments and feedback on the various edits and maquettes I have produced over the years.

Heathcote Williams, Rory Carnegie, Xa Sturgis and Peter Hamilton for their interesting and generous written responses to the work.

Toby Matthews for the cover design and his valuable contribution to the final editing and sequence of the book.

Amy Bleasdale for her editing, management and comments.

David Alan Harvey and Michael Akerman for helping me find my photographic path.

Heulwen and my amazing children Kristoffer, Anna and Oscar.

James A. Hudson
August 2015

PATRONS

This book was only made possible with the generous support of the following people:

Abby, Beth & Carla Stafford
Adam Stirling
Amy Bleasdale
Andrew Turner
Andy Cawley
Anthony Aris
Arabella & Chris Hobson
Babette Kulik
Bob Marsden
Bonnie T. Marques
Brynmor Davies
Chris & Sue Hudson
Chris Goddard
Clare Bernadette Downy
Darrell Shrubb
David Vernon Bloxam
Dr. Bryony Alexandra Stott
Eirys Morgan
Ellen & Ben Howey
Frances Reed
Henry, Alexandra & Catherine Margaret Kim
Irmgard Hüppe & Simon Murison-Bowie

Ieuan Davies
James Arrowsmith
Jen Phillips
Joanne Payan
Joe & Ann Robbins
John Hudson
John Ruddock
Judith Barber
Julian G.S. James
Keith Davies
Kelly Murphy
Kev Firth
Lindy Mason & Holly Mason-Franchitti
Longstone Tyres
Matthew Worland
Matthieu Williams
Max Hamilton
Mini Grey & Tony Langtry
Morten Brakestad
Nicola Hudson
Paddy Summerfield
Patricia Baker-Cassidy

Peter & Linda Bulloch
Peter Jennison
Polly & Pierre
RAW Architecture
Richard Sidwell & Penny Harding
Rick Mather Architects
Rob Lancefield
Rodrigo Arce
Rosemary Godfrey & Jeff Davies
Ruth Charity
Ruth, Michael, Jasper & Felix Hudson
Sarah Price
Siriol Davies
Steven Church
Steven Jackson
Sunil Shah
T.R. Hughes
The Robbins Family
Thomas Sund
Tom Robbins

This edition published in 2015 by

The Bardwell Press
Tithe Barn House, 11 High Street, Cumnor, Oxford, OX2 9PE
www.bardwell-press.co.uk

Photography © 2015 James A. Hudson
Text © 2015 James A. Hudson, Peter Hamilton, Xa Sturgis

This book is number ....**36**.... of a limited edition of ....**350**.... individually numbered copies

ISBN 978-1-905622-52-8

A catalogue record for this publication is available from the British Library.

Designed by Toby Matthews
Typeset by The Bardwell Press, Oxford

Printed in Italy by Graphicom